びわ湖は薬師如来の池とされ、日本仏教の母山など多くの寺社は人々の信仰を集めてきた。戦国武将は水運を重視し、その環境は近江商人を生み出した。また、水の恵みを受け、水を汚さない循環の知恵が暮らしのなかに伝わっている。水と人の営みが調和した「滋賀・びわ湖」へようこそ。

Lake Biwa has long garnered the faith of many for its association with Yakushi Nyorai (Buddha of Healing) and the numerous temples and shrines along its shores, including the mountaintop monastery that fathered Japanese Buddhism. Military commanders during Japan's Age of Civil Wars (1467 - 1590) saw the lake's importance for transportation and the business-savvy merchants of Omi capitalized on the infrastructure they built to conduct lucrative trade across the country. Moreover, the lake's natural blessings spawned the insight and wisdom to keep the water clean by circulation -- know-how that has been passed down through the ages as an integral part of daily life. Welcome to Lake Biwa where people have honed a way of life in harmony with nature.

滋賀・びわ湖
水辺の祈りと暮らし

Lake Biwa, Shiga
Worship and Life at Water's Edge

淡海(おうみ)文化を育てる会 編　辻村耕司 撮影

Edited by the
Omi Culture Supporters' Club

Photographs by
Tsujimura Koji

湧き水を飲料水や生活水として利用する「カバタ」（高島市新旭町針江）
Kabata, a system of wells, canals and conduits for using spring water for drinking, washing, etc. (Harie, Shin'asahicho, Takashima City)

目　次

一、琵琶湖は天台薬師の池⋯⋯⋯⋯⋯⋯⋯⋯ 6
　　　白鬚神社／浮御堂（満月寺）
　　　日本仏教の発祥地⋯⋯⋯⋯⋯⋯⋯⋯⋯ 12
　　　比叡山延暦寺／園城寺（三井寺）／西教寺
　　コラム●水を愛でる①　里坊の暮らし⋯⋯ 20

二、天下の平安祈願⋯⋯⋯⋯⋯⋯⋯⋯⋯⋯ 22
　　　神の水に感謝／八ヶ崎神事／日吉山王祭／
　　　葛川明王院の太鼓回し／比良八講
　　コラム●比叡山の回峰行⋯⋯⋯⋯⋯⋯⋯ 34
　　　琵琶湖の観音信仰⋯⋯⋯⋯⋯⋯⋯⋯⋯ 36
　　　竹生島／長命寺／観音正寺／石山寺／
　　　正法寺（岩間寺）／園城寺（三井寺）
　　コラム●水を愛でる②　大名庭園⋯⋯⋯⋯ 50

三、水運を重視した武将たち⋯⋯⋯⋯⋯⋯ 52
　　　大溝城／安土城／伊庭

四、近江商人を生んだ水環境⋯⋯⋯⋯⋯⋯ 68
　　　西の湖／八幡堀／五個荘金堂

五、湖畔に生きる⋯⋯⋯⋯⋯⋯⋯⋯⋯⋯⋯ 78
　　　海津・西浜・知内／針江・霜降／菅浦／沖島
　　コラム●古写真に見る湖畔の人々の暮らし⋯ 82
　　コラム●琵琶湖八珍⋯⋯⋯⋯⋯⋯⋯⋯⋯ 96

六、水系に暮らす⋯⋯⋯⋯⋯⋯⋯⋯⋯⋯⋯ 98
　　　高時川／姉川／愛知川／野洲川／安曇川／醒井宿
　　コラム●雨乞い御礼の太鼓踊り⋯⋯⋯⋯ 102
　　コラム●滋賀の名水⋯⋯⋯⋯⋯⋯⋯⋯ 118

七、琵琶湖の源流⋯⋯⋯⋯⋯⋯⋯⋯⋯⋯ 120

滋賀・びわ湖に行こう【本書で紹介した滋賀の日本遺産】⋯⋯ 124

長浜市

p.101 ■東草野の山村景観

■海津・西浜・知内の水辺景観 p.80　■p.88 菅浦の湖岸集落景観

p.122 ■伊吹山西麓地域

p.38 竹生島

高島市

p.102 朝日豊年太鼓踊および伊吹山麓の太鼓踊と奉納神社

シコブチ信仰 p.112 ■

p.84 針江・霜降の水辺景観

米原市　■p.114 醒井宿

大溝の水辺景観 p.56 ■

玄宮楽々園 p.50 ■　p.51 旧彦根藩松原下屋敷（お浜御殿）庭園

白鬚神社 p.8 ■　彦根城

p.22 伊崎寺　彦根市

沖島 p.92 ■　p.64 伊庭の水辺景観

長命寺 p.40 ■　p.74 五個荘金堂

近江八幡市

p.68 近江八幡の水郷

西教寺 p.18 ■　大津市　p.104 永源寺と奥永源寺の山村景観

p.10 浮御堂（満月寺）

p.14 ■ p.28 日吉大社　東近江市

比叡山延暦寺

p.16, p.48 ■ 園城寺（三井寺）

p.24 建部大社

p.44 石山寺

本書で紹介した滋賀の日本遺産

Contents

1. **The Lake of the Tendai Buddha of Healing** 6
   Shirahigejinja Shrine / Ukimido (Mangetsuji) Temple
   The Birthplace of Japanese Buddhism 12
   Enryakuji Temple on Mt. Hiei / Onjoji (Miidera) Temple / Saikyoji Temple

   column Attracted to Water [1] • Life in a Satobo 20

2. **Prayers for Peace on Earth** 22
   Thankful to the God of Water / Hachigasakishinji /
   Parade of Boats in the Hiyoshisannosai /
   Taikomawashi at Katsuragawamyooin Temple / Hirahakko

   column • Kaihogyo of Mt. Hiei 34

   Reverence of the Goddess of Mercy Around Lake Biwa 36
   Chikubushima Island / Chomeiji Temple / Kannonshoji Temple /
   Ishiyamadera Temple / Shoboji (Iwamadera) Temple /
   Onjoji (Miidera) Temple

   column Attracted to Water [2] • Gardens of the Daimyos 50

3. **The Importance of Water for Transportation** 52
   Omizo Castle / Azuchi Castle / Iba

4. **A Water Environment That Spurred Trade in Omi** ... 68
   Lake Nishinoko / Hachimanhori / Gokashokondocho

5. **Living Lakeside** 78
   Kaizu • Nishihama • Chinai • Harie • Shimofuri • Sugaura • Okishima

   column • Old Photos of Life Along the Shores of Lake Biwa 82
   column • 8 Gastronomic Delicacies from Lake Biwa 96

6. **Life Along Lake Biwa's Feeder Rivers** 98
   Takatoki River / Ane River / Echi River / Yasu River / Ado River /
   Samegaishuku

   column • Rain Dancing to the Beat of Drums 102
   column • Prized Water Sources in Shiga 118

7. **Headwaters** 120

Let's go to Lake Biwa 【Information on placement place】 124

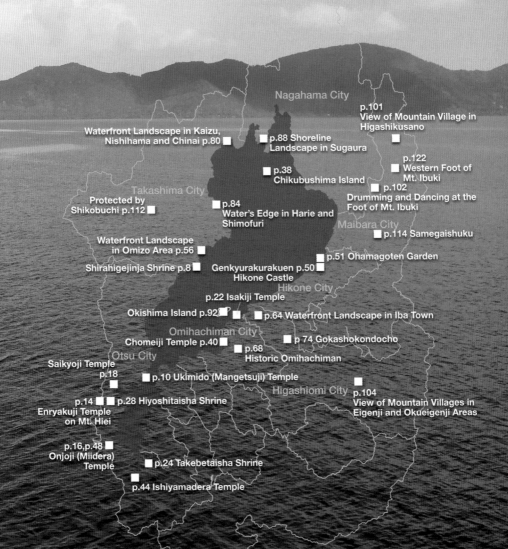

Japan Heritages in Shiga introduced in this book

一、琵琶湖は天台薬師の池

1. The Lake of the Tendai Buddha of Healing

「近江の湖は海ならず、天台薬師の池ぞかし、何ぞの海、常楽我浄の風吹けば、七宝蓮華の波ぞ立つ」(『梁塵秘抄』第二より)

"Lake Biwa is not an ocean, but the east lake of the pure lazuli land where Bhaisajyaguru, the healing Buddha of the Tendai sect able to cure all ills, resides, and when the winds of Sukhavati (Amitabha's Pure Land) blow, waves like lotus leaves sparkling like the seven treasures (gold, silver, pearls, agate, crystal, coral, lapis lazuli) arise." (2nd verse of "Ryojin Hisho (Songs to Make the Dust Dance)"

白鬚神社 Shirahigejinja Shrine

　高島市鵜川(うかわ)の白鬚神社のもともとの祭神は、「琵琶湖が芦原になるのを7度見た。6万年もの間、比良(ひら)に住んでいた」長寿の神だという。湖中に立つ大鳥居から「近江の厳島(いつくしま)」とも呼ばれている。

The deity revered at Shirahigejinja in Ukawa, Takashima City is said to have "seen Lake Biwa change to a reed field seven times, and lived on Mt. Hira for 60,000 years". Because of the large Shinto arch that stands in the lake, the shrine is often dubbed the "Itsukushima of Omi" in reference to the renown shrine on Miyajima Island that similarly has an arch offshore.

境内には白鬚神社の情景を愛でた紫式部や松尾芭蕉、与謝野晶子の句歌碑が見られる
On the shrine's grounds are found stones etched with waka poems composed by Murasaki Shikibu (978 – 1016), Matsuo Basho (1644 – 1694) and Yosano Akiko (1878 – 1942), all of who adored the shrine's landscape.

白鬚神社は全国に分布する白鬚社の総本社とされる
Shirahigejinja is the headquarters of similarly named subordinate shrines scattered across Japan.

近江八景の一つ「堅田の落雁」で知られる浮御堂
Ukimido Temple was made known through the woodblock print "Descending Geese in Katata" that was painted by Utagawa Hiroshige (1797 – 1858) as one of his "8 Views of Omi" series.

お堂の中に安置されている千体阿弥陀仏
1,000 figurines of Amidabutsu inside of Ukimido Temple

浮御堂(満月寺)

Ukimido (Mangetsuji) Temple

　大津市堅田の湖中に突き出した堂宇が特徴の浮御堂（満月寺）は、平安時代、恵心僧都源信が、湖上通船の安全と衆生済度を念じて建立し、千体阿弥陀仏を安置したことに始まると伝わる。堂宇に火が灯れば湖上をゆく船の灯台となったことだろう。

Built over the lake off the shoreline in Katata, Otsu City, Ukimido (Mangetsuji) was reportedly erected by the Tendai scholar and cleric Sozu Eshin (942 – 1017) and stocked with 1,000 figurines of Amidabutsu in the Heian Period (794 - 1185) to pray for safe navigation on the lake and to guide the masses on the path to Buddhist enlightenment. It likely was lit up with torches in order to function as a lighthouse.

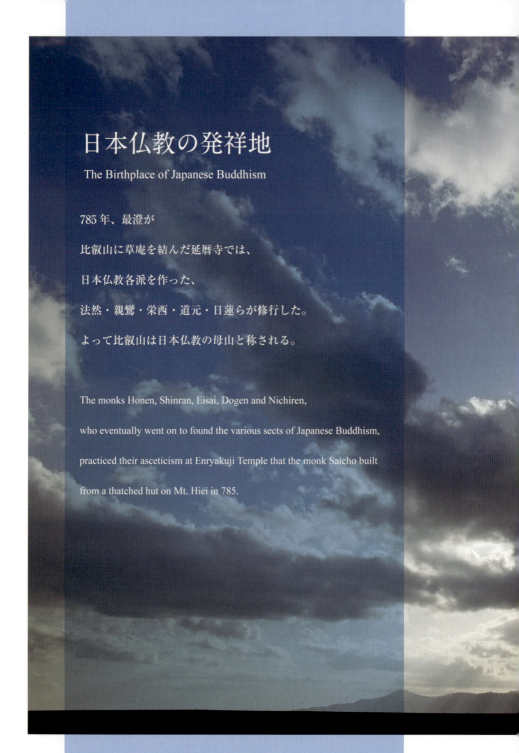

日本仏教の発祥地
The Birthplace of Japanese Buddhism

785年、最澄が

比叡山に草庵を結んだ延暦寺では、

日本仏教各派を作った、

法然・親鸞・栄西・道元・日蓮らが修行した。

よって比叡山は日本仏教の母山と称される。

The monks Honen, Shinran, Eisai, Dogen and Nichiren,

who eventually went on to found the various sects of Japanese Buddhism,

practiced their asceticism at Enryakuji Temple that the monk Saicho built

from a thatched hut on Mt. Hiei in 785.

琵琶湖東岸、野洲川付近から比叡山を望む
Mt. Hiei seen from the east bank of Lake Biwa near the Yasu River

最澄が結んだ草庵・一乗止観院を受け継ぐ根本中堂
Konponchudo Temple replaced the thatched hut built and named "Ichijoshikan' in" by the monk Saicho.

1200年以上にわたって守り継がれているという根本中堂内陣の「不滅の法灯」
"Eternal Lanterns" have safeguarded the inner sanctuary of Konponchudo Temple for over 1,200 years.

比叡山延暦寺
Enryakuji Temple on Mt. Hiei

　最澄が比叡山に開いた天台宗総本山で、世界文化遺産。眼下に琵琶湖を望む山全体が聖域であり、東塔・西塔・横川の三つの地域に多くの堂塔伽藍が建ち並ぶ。（大津市坂本本町）

Enryakuji is the head temple of Tendai Buddhism that the monk Saicho launched on Mt. Hiei. It is also a UNESCO World Heritage Site. With its panoramic view of Lake Biwa below, the entire mountain is hallowed ground. The monastery itself is divided into three zones – Todo, Saito and Yokawa – that are home to numerous temples, pagodas and halls. (Sakamotohonmachi, Otsu City)

根本中堂付近に立つ最澄幼年像
Statue of a young Saicho located near Konponchudo Temple

比叡山の北に立つ横川中堂
Yokawachudo Temple on the northern end of Mt. Hiei

一、琵琶湖は天台薬師の池　　15

三井の霊泉
"Mii" sacred spring

園城寺（三井寺） Onjoji (Miidera) Temple

　大津市園城寺町の三井寺には、天智・天武・持統の古代三帝の産湯に用いられたとされる霊泉の閼伽井があり、平安時代前期にこの水を智証大師が天台儀式の法水に用いたことから「御井寺」「三井寺」と呼ばれるようになったという。

On the grounds of Miidera in Onjojicho, Otsu City is found a well to a sacred spring whose water was used for the births of the Emperors Tenji (626 – 672) and Tenmu (631? – 686) and the Empress Jito (645 – 703). The temple is said to have gotten its name, which depending on the characters can mean a "holy well" or "three wells", from stories that the monk Chisho (814 – 891) had used its water for rituals practiced in Tendai Buddhism in the early Heian Period.

霊泉を覆う閼伽井屋
Well house built over the sacred spring

国宝の金堂は、桃山時代を代表する天台系本堂の古式を伝える建築
Designated a National Treasure, Kondo Temple is a classic example of the architectural styling used for important temples built in the Momoyama Period (1568 – 1600) by the Tendai Sect of Buddhism.

西教寺 Saikyoji Temple

　大津市坂本の西教寺は、聖徳太子が創建し、真盛上人が不断念仏道場として復興した天台三総本山の一つ。琵琶湖を東方浄土の極楽の池、天台薬師の池と見る「水の浄土」の信仰を集める。

Located in Sakamoto, Otsu City, Saikyoji was originally built by the Prince Shotoku (574 – 622) and later converted into a dojo for chanting by the monk Shinsei (1443 – 1495). It functions as one of the three head temples of Tendai Buddhism. The temple earned a following as a "paradise" because of its view of Lake Biwa, which was treated as belonging to the Eastern Pure Land and considered the lake of the Tendai Buddha of Healing.

書院の庭には琵琶湖の形をした池があり、湖と祈りが結びついた景観を伝える
The pond in the garden off the lecture hall is shaped like Lake Biwa and was reportedly landscaped to establish a connection between the lake and worship.

平安時代から栽培されている食用の「坂本菊」
Edible Sakamoto chrysanthemums have been grown and harvested since the Heian Period (794 - 1185).

西教寺のひな祭りの雛御膳
Hinagozen served at Saikyoji Temple during the Hinamatsuri (Doll Festival)

一、琵琶湖は天台薬師の池

水を愛でる①　●里坊の暮らし　Attracted to Water [1] • Life in a Satobo

滋賀院の庭園
Garden at Shigain Temple

盛安寺客殿
Reception hall at Seianji Temple

　重要伝統的建造物群保存地区である比叡山麓の坂本のまちは、石垣と生垣、土塀に囲まれた延暦寺の里坊が点在する。山上で修行を積んだ老僧が座主より里坊を賜って居住したことに始まり、それぞれの里坊には、山から流れ出る水を利用した風雅な庭園がある。厳しい修行を終えた老僧がここで静かに暮らす。

Spread across the skirt of Mt. Hiei, Sakamoto is designated an Important Preservation District of Historic Buildings because of the idyllic landscape created by the homes enclosed in stone revetments, hedges and mud walls. Known as satobo, these residences were awarded by the head priest of Enryakuji Temple to senior monks after completing their rigorous training on the mountain so that they could lead a quiet life. Each of the residences has an attentively groomed garden fed with water from the mountain.

二、天下の平安祈願

2. Prayers for Peace on Earth

琵琶湖に飛び込む行者
Ascetics taking a leap of faith into Lake Biwa

近江八幡市白王町の伊崎寺から琵琶湖に突き出た十数メートルの棹から湖中に飛び込む「伊崎の棹とび」は、毎年8月1日の千日会に行われる「捨身の業」と呼ばれる修行。行者は人々のさまざまな願いを背負い、わが身を捨ててその成就のために飛び込むという。当日は本堂で百日回峰行者が出仕して大般若経の転読が行われ、続いて棹とびとなる。

Every year on August 1, a peculiar "sacrificial" ritual known as Izakinosaotobi takes place at Isakiji Temple in Shiraocho, Omihachiman City. Entrusted with the prayers of others, ascetics jump from a plank over 10 m high into Lake Biwa as a gesture of their renouncing the flesh for the greater good. Prior to the jumping, practitioners on a 100-Day Circumambulation transcribe the Great Perfection of Wisdom Sutra at the temple's main hall of worship.

水の神に感謝 Thankful to the God of Water

　琵琶湖から流れ出る唯一の天然河川・瀬田川で行われる船幸祭(せんこうさい)は建部大社(たけべ)(大津市神領)の夏の祭礼で、夕刻、神輿(みこし)を和船に乗せて黒津の旅所に向かい、戻ってくる夜半には賑やかな花火の競演が始まる。

As the only natural river flowing into Lake Biwa, the Seta River sets the stage for a fortuitous summertime celebration hosted by Takebetaisha Shrine in Jinryo, Otsu City. Known as Senkosai, the festivities start at sunset with portable alters set adrift on rafts towards their resting place during the festival in Kurozu. Their midnight arrival is greeted with an exciting show of fireworks.

神霊を移した神輿が船に乗せられ瀬田川を下る
Portable alters for transporting divine spirits are set afloat on the Seta River.

近江八景の一つ「唐崎の夜雨」で知られる唐崎神社(大津市唐崎)の夏越神事では、古いお札やお守りを清める湖上焚上げ神事が行われる。湖上で焚くことで神に祈りを届けるという

Old amulets and talismans are purified by setting them afire on Lake Biwa during the Nagoshishinji ceremony performed at Karasakijinja Shrine in Karasaki, Otsu City. The prayers and wishes they embody are carried to the gods by the smoke. The shrine itself was made famous by the woodblock print "Evening Rain in Karasaki" that was painted by Utagawa Hiroshige (1797 – 1858) as one of his "8 Views of Omi" series.

大津市和邇で行われる和邇祭は五つの集落ごとの神輿が琵琶湖岸に勢ぞろいする
Portable Shinto alters from 5 villages lined up along the shore of Lake Biwa in Wai, Otsu City for the springtime festival known as Wanisai.

八坂神社（甲賀市水口町嶬峨）の春祭りでは野洲川本流を勇壮に渡御する
Parishioners carrying a portable Shinto alter across the main stream of the Yasu River as part of the springtime festival hosted by Yasakajinja Shrine in Gika, Minakuchicho, Koka City.

八ヶ崎神事 Hachigasakishinji

野洲市五条の兵主大社祭神の兵主神は対岸の大津市穴太から白蛇に姿を変えて亀の甲に乗って琵琶湖を渡り、鹿の群れに守られながら現在の場所に着いたという。宮司が琵琶湖に入り、ご神体を水に浸して、神威の復活を祈る「八ヶ崎神事」が行われる。

Legend has it that the deity of Hyozutaisha Shrine in Gojo, Yasu City transformed himself into a white snake and rode across Lake Biwa on the back of a turtle from Otsu City on the opposite bank. Protected by a herd of deer, he chose to settle in the shrine's current location. As part of the Hachigasakishinji, the head priest from the shrine immerses sacred idols in the lake to rejuvenate their power.

兵主大社の楼門　Main gate to Hyozutaisha Shrine

粟津御供といわれる琵琶湖上での神事
Foods being tossed in Lake Biwa to appease the gods

日吉大社(大津市坂本)境内
Procession at Hiyoshitaisha Shrine in Sakamoto, Otsu City

日吉大社の紅葉
Hiyoshitaisha Shrine under the autumnal foliage

日吉山王祭船渡御 Parade of Boats in the Hiyoshisannosai

　1ヶ月半にも及ぶ日吉山王祭は、男女神の聖婚を表わすといわれる。琵琶湖に7基の神輿が繰り出す船渡御では、琵琶湖上を唐崎沖まで進むと、船上に供える粟津御供が惜しげもなく湖に投げ入れられる。これは、大津宮の守護神が琵琶湖に渡ってきた時、漁夫が粟飯を差し上げたことに由来し、琵琶湖の神に直接お供えする神事として伝わる。

Celebrated over a month-and-a-half period, the Hiyoshisannosai consists of a series of rituals and events said to represent the holy matrimony between gods. In the procession of boats, 7 portable Shinto alters are paraded on Lake Biwa to a point off of Karasaki where specially prepared festive foods are unsparingly thrown into the water. The festival is said to have originated from fishermen offering boiled rice with millet to the tutelary god of the imperial palace of the Emperor Tenji (626 – 672) in Otsu after crossing Lake Biwa, and has been continued as a Shinto ritual for making direct offerings to the gods of the lake.

撮影：山口幸次　Photo courtesy of Yamaguchi Yukitsugu

結婚した男女神の御子神誕生を表わす勇壮な午の神事
Thrilling action during the Umanoshinji ritual celebrating the birth of a son to the newly married gods

葛川明王院の太鼓回し
Taikomawashi at Katsuragawamyooin Temple

　大津市葛川坊村町の葛川明王院は、求道のための土地を探していた相応が庵での参籠後、満願の日に滝壺に飛び込み、ここから引き揚げた霊木に不動明王を刻んで安置したことに始まり、室町時代には足利義尚や日野富子が参籠したことを示す参籠札が残る。太鼓回しは天台回峰行の夏安居の行事で、この後、明王院東側の三ノ滝で修行し5日間の行事が終わる。

Katsuragawamyooin Temple in Katsuragawabomuracho, Otsu City has its beginning when, out searching for a place from where he could seek the truth, the monk Soo immersed himself in prayer and meditation inside a hut. After fulfilling his vows, he allegedly dove into the pool at the base of a nearby waterfall and pulled from the water a sacred tree from which he then carved a figure of the God of Fire that served as the temple's centerpiece. Today, the temple preserves the prayer slats of the Shogun Ashikaga Yoshihisa (1465 – 1489) and Hino Tomiko (1440 – 1496). The Taikomawashi is a 5-day ritual held at a summer retreat by Tendai monks that involves spinning a large drum in turns and jumping on it when it stops. The activities climax with chanting under the Sanno Falls on the eastern side of the temple.

行者が修行する三ノ滝
Sanno Falls where the monks do their chanting

葛川明王院を開いた相応が滝に飛び込む様子を表しているとされる「太鼓回し」
A monk prepared to dive on the large drum in the Taikomawashi. Presumably, the act represents the monk Soo's dive into the waterfall, which led to him to building the temple.

堂内の参籠札
Prayer slats inside the temple

大津港を出港した船上から、蓬莱山で取水した「法水」を琵琶湖にそそぎ湖水の清浄を祈願した後、湖上に御札を投げ入れ航行の安全を祈る
After departing Otsu Port, monks pour holy water they collected on Mt. Horaisan into Lake Biwa to purify the lake. Following that, they toss prayer sheets from the ship to ask for safe navigation.

比良八講 Hirahakko

　冬から春にかけて比良山からの突風が吹き荒れることを「比良八荒」といい、人々は「比良八荒あれじまい」といって春の到来を待つ。かつて天台の宗教行事として五穀豊穣や風雨順時を祈った法華八講法会が「比良八講」の起源とされ、1955年に比叡山の箱崎文応大阿闍梨が現在の形に整えた。

The gusts of wind that blow off Mt. Hira in late March are called Hirahakko and signal the coming of spring. This name comes from a 4-day service of the same pronunciation performed in Tendai Buddhism to pray for rain and a good harvest. The current format was engineered in 1955 by Daiajari Hakozaki Bun'o.

水難者の回向と湖上の安全を祈願する雄松崎での護摩法要
Memorial bonfire in Omatsuzaki to pray for safety on the lake and honor those who drowned

●比叡山の回峰行 • Kaihogyo of Mt. Hiei

千日回峰行に挑む藤波源信阿闍梨
Ajari Fujinami Genshin on his 1000-Day Circumambulation

回峰行(かいほうぎょう)は、毎日休むことなく比叡の峰を巡り歩く修行であり、百日回峰行の最後が葛川参籠（p.30 参照）であるが、さらに7年間を要する千日回峰行は修行中最大の荒行といえる。七百日を満行すると阿闍梨と呼ばれるようになり、千日満行すると大阿闍梨と尊称される。

The Kaihogyo is a 100-day non-stop circumambulation of the peaks of Mt. Hiei that culminates with immersion in prayer and meditation at Katsuragawamyooin Temple (see pg. 30). It is also said to be the most rigorous segment of ascetic training in the 1000-Day Circumambulation that requires 7 years to complete. Practitioners who complete 700 days are given the honorific title of Ajari, while those who make it the whole 1000 days are called Daiajari.

はきつぶされた草履
Worn-out straw sandals

山中を行く藤波源信阿闍梨
Ajari Fujinami Genshin trekking in the mountains

琵琶湖の観音信仰
Reverence of the Goddess of Mercy Around Lake Biwa

滋賀県は古くから「仏の国」といわれ、
多くの仏像があり、優れたものが多い。
井上靖の『星と祭』で全国的に有名になった湖北の観音像は、
戦火のなか地域の人々が守り続け、
今も村人たちの献身的な信仰心に支えられている。
一方、2018年で草創1300年の西国三十三所観音巡礼の札所は
県内に6ヶ所あり、いずれもが名刹である。

A long time ago, Shiga Prefecture was referred to as the "Land of Buddha". There are numerous statues of Buddha across the prefecture, many of which are exemplar works of art. One particular statue of the Goddess of Mercy * found in the northern end of the lake was made famous all across Japan in the novel "Hoshi to Matsuri" by Inoue Yasushi (1907 – 1991) that recounts how local villagers protected her through the fires of war. She is cared for still today by the devoted spirit of the villagers.

As a side note, there are 6 temples in Shiga Prefecture that count amongst the 33 points of worship of the Shikoku 33 Circumambulation, which marks its 1300th anniversary in 2018. All 6 are reputed and renown.

* Said Kannon in Japanese.

琵琶湖に浮かぶ竹生島
Chikubushima Island in Lake Biwa

琵琶湖から竹生島港をのぞむ
Chikubushima harbor seen from Lake Biwa

水神を崇めるパワースポット
竹生島宝厳寺

Fear and Veneration of the Goddess of Water
Hogonji Temple, Chikubushima Island

　奈良時代、聖武天皇の発願で行基が島に渡り、弁才天と千手千顔観音を祀ったことによって開かれ、日本で最初に弁才天信仰が根付いた。古来、浅井姫命が鎮座し、水神として崇められ、付近を航行する船を守る神として信仰を集める。近年はパワースポットとして名高い。(長浜市早崎町)

　Worship of the Goddess of Water in Japan began in the Nara Period, when, at the request of Emperor Shomu (701 - 756), the monk Gyoki made the crossing to Chikubushima Island and built this temple to honor Benzaiten and the Kannon of 1,000 Arms and Eyes. Long before that, the Shinto deity Azaihime was enshrined in the island and revered as the Goddess of Water, which many equate to safeguarding boats navigating the nearby waters. In recent years, the temple has earned a name as a spiritually uplifting location that harbors mystical energy. (Hayazakicho, Nagahama City)

琵琶湖に突き出る都久夫須麻神社拝殿の鳥居
Shinto arch belonging to Tsukubusumajinja Shrine that leads to a point of worship jutting out into Lake Biwa

宝厳寺本堂（弁才天堂）内
Inside Hogonji (Benzaitendo) Temple

本堂や三重塔など、国の重要文化財を多く有する
The main hall and 3-tier pagoda are two of the nationally designated Important Cultural Properties at Chomeiji Temple.

水の浄土信仰・長命寺
Finding a Spiritual Element in Water at Chomeiji Temple

琵琶湖を見下ろす景勝地に築かれた西国三十三所 31 番札所。不動の滝など水の浄土信仰を表わすところとして知られ、秘仏の薬師如来像が祀られる。（近江八幡市長命寺町）

Built in a scenic location with a commanding view over Lake Biwa, Chomeiji Temple is the 31st point of worship on the Shikoku 33 Circumambulation. Because of the nearby Fudo Falls and other "watery" associations, the temple is known as an epicenter for stirring belief of a spiritual element in water's purity. Inside, there is a statue of Yakushi Nyorai (Buddha of Healing) of Esoteric Buddhism. (Chomeijicho, Omihachiman City)

上空から長命寺山と琵琶湖、沖島を望む
Arial view of Mt. Chomeiji, Lake Biwa and Okishima Island

アジサイに包まれ 808 段の長い階段が続く
808-step stairway bordered by hydrangeas

人魚伝説が伝わる観音正寺

Kannonshoji Temple

　観音正寺本堂に至る標高362mの険しい山道は、西国三十三所一番の難所といわれるが、ここからの近江平野の眺めは見事。1993年に本堂と本尊を焼失したが、1998年に新たに白檀で造った総高6mの千手観音坐像が安置された。寺には人魚伝説が伝わる。（近江八幡市安土町石寺）

The steep path up to the main hall at Kannonshoji Temple is said to be the most treacherous segment of the Shikoku 33 Circumambulation, but the view of the Omi Plains from the 362 m elevation is absolutely worth the climb. The main hall and its statue of Buddha were destroyed by fire in 1993, but a 6 m tall sandalwood statue of the sitting 1,000-Arm Kannon was newly erected in 1998. Kannonshoji is also associated with legends of mermaids. (Azuchicho Ishidera, Omihachiman City)

繖山中腹の観音正寺
Temple garden located halfway up Mt. Kinugasa

1998年に開眼式が行われた白檀の千手観音坐像
Sandalwood statue of a sitting 1,000-Arm Kannon that was consecrated in 1998

月の名所・石山寺 Great Spot for Moon Watching, Ishiyamadera Temple

　平安時代、京の都から石山寺に多くの人が参詣した。その中の一人紫式部は、十五夜の月が琵琶湖に映える姿を見て「もののあわれ」を主題とする『源氏物語』を着想したと伝わる。西国三十三所13番札所。本尊の如意輪観音は秘仏で33年に一度、開帳される。（大津市石山寺）

During the Heian Period (794 – 1185), many people made the pilgrimage from Kyoto to Ishiyamadera Temple. It is told that one such person, Murasaki Shikibu (978 – 1016), came up with the storyline of human pathos for "The Tale of Genji" after seeing the full moon reflected off Lake Biwa here. The temple is the 13th point of worship on the Saigoku 33 Circumambulation. The principle idol of the temple is Nyoirin Kannon (Bodhisattva of Compassion) and, because of the temple's affiliation with Esoteric Buddhism, the statue is opened to public viewing only once every 33 years. (Ishiyamadera, Otsu City)

瀬田川から見る石山寺。四季折々の変化を見せる
Ishiyamadera Temple seen from the Seta River. The temple grounds and surroundings beautifully manifest the changing seasons.

天然記念物の硅灰岩の奥に多宝塔が見える
The temple's 2-tiered pagoda can be spotted behind the exposed wollastonite bedrock that is designated a National Monument.

石山寺で『源氏物語』を着想した紫式部の像
Statue of Murasaki Shikibu. The poetess conceived the plot for "The Tale of Genji" at Ishiyamadera Temple.

芭蕉の発句で知られる正法寺(岩間寺)
From a Poem by Basho, Shohoji (Iwamadera) Temple

水不足になった時、開祖・泰澄大師が雨乞いの祈願を行うと大きな落雷があり、さらに落雷を収める祈祷を続けたところ、雷が「大師の弟子になりたい」と言い、これまでの悪行を反省して水不足に悩む人々のために自らの爪で岩を掘ると水が湧き出たという。(大津市石山内畑町)

When the local area was hit by drought, the priest Taicho (682 – 767) who built Iwamadera Temple prayed for rain. A large thunderbolt rang from the sky, so he prayed for more. Regretting the pain he inflicted on mankind by causing the drought, the God of Thunder sought to learn from the priest and, as a gesture of remorse, dug through the rocks with his fingers until water sprang from the earth. (Ishiyamauchihatacho, Otsu City)

芭蕉真筆の「古池や蛙飛び込む水の音」の碑
Monument to Basho's internationally renowned haiku "An old pond / A frog jumps / The sound of water"

不動明王を祀る不動堂
Fudodo Temple that venerates the God of Fire, Fudomyoo

芭蕉の句にちなむ「蛙池」
Pond referenced by Basho in his famous haiku about a frog

琵琶湖から京都にそそぐ琵琶湖疏水
Canal that flows from Lake Biwa to Kyoto

本尊の水観音を祀る園城寺(三井寺)
Venerating the Kannon of Water, Onjoji (Miidera) Temple

　西国三十三所14番札所であると同時に、西国薬師霊場48番札所でもあり、水観音といわれる本尊の薬師如来は、極楽浄土への信仰対象として人々の崇敬を集める。(大津市園城寺町)

Onjoji Temple is both the 14th point of worship on the Saigoku 33 Circumambulation and the 48th point of worship on the Saigoku Yakushi Pilgrimage. The temple venerates Yakushi Nyorai as the Kannon of Water. She draws reverence from the public by inspiring the faithful to pursue nirvana. (Onjojicho, Otsu City)

園城寺(三井寺)の観音堂
Kannondo of Onjoji (Miidera)

水を愛でる② ●大名庭園（玄宮楽々園・お浜御殿）
Attracted to Water [2] • Gardens of the Daimyos (Genkyurakuen and Ohamagoten)

雪の玄宮園。彦根城天守がその奥に見える
Genkyuen under the snow. The main tower of Hikone Castle can be seen in the background.

玄宮園は、彦根藩４代藩主・井伊直興が下屋敷として作った楽々園に隣接する大名庭園。国宝彦根城天守を借景とする池泉回遊式庭園で、玄宗皇帝の離宮にちなんで命名された。池は城下の湧水を外堀からサイフォンの原理で導入し、小島の岩間から水を落として滝に仕立てるなど、水を巧みに取り入れている。（彦根市金亀町）

The Genkyuen is a garden of the aristocracy, built next to a similar garden known as "Rakurakuen" by the 4th generation castle lord, Ii Naooki (1656 – 1717), as a villa. Designed with paths around a central pond, the gardens incorporate the main tower of Hikone Castle, a National Treasure, into the landscape. The name was taken from a second palace used by the Emperor Genso. Ingenuity was used to introduce water by siphoning spring water from the castle's outer moat and creating waterfalls between the rocks that serve as islands. (Konkicho, Hikone City)

四季それぞれの美しさを見せる玄宮園（彦根市金亀町）
Genkyuen portrays the beauty of the changing seasons. (Konkicho, Hikone City)

「お浜御殿」と呼ばれる旧彦根藩松原下屋敷。池泉回遊式庭園で、琵琶湖の水位と連動して波打ち際が変化する汐入り方式。淡水を利用したものとしては国内で唯一（彦根市松原町）

The "Ohamagoten" was where the former lord Matsubara of Hikone Castle had his residence. These gardens, too, are designed with paths around a central pond, but because it is fed by Lake Biwa, the water level rises and lowers notably along its banks. It is the only garden in Japan to employ the tidal action of a fresh water lake. (Matsubaracho, Hikone City)

三、水運を重視した武将たち

3. The Importance of Water for Transportation

　　武家の頂点に立った織田信長は1576年、天下統一の拠点とするべく安土での築城に着手した。安土は、近江を縦横に走る街道と琵琶湖の存在を活かした水陸交通の要衝（ようしょう）であり、軍略上きわめて重要な位置にあった。安土城のほか既存の佐和山城を含め、北に長浜城、対岸に大溝（みぞ）城、京都近くに坂本城を築城していった。信長なき後、秀吉もその軍略を重視し、秀次が近江八幡に八幡山城を築き、琵琶湖から内湖（ないこ）を通じる掘割を開いた。

織田信澄が築いた大溝城に隣接する乙女ヶ池(高島市勝野)。周辺は古代よりの良港で万葉集にも多く詠まれる

Lake Otomegaike was next to Omizo Castle that was built by Oda Nobuzumi (1555? – 1582) (Katsuno, Takashima City). Because of the natural port nearby, the lake appears often in the Man'yo Verses.

Standing at the top of the warrior class of Japan, Oda Nobunaga built a castle in Azuchi from where he would unify the country, in 1576. From a military perspective, Azuchi was strategically located owing to the ancient roads that crossed Omi and inland transportation routes that utilized Lake Biwa. Other castles besides Azuchi Castle were built on the lake like the previously existing Sawayama Castle, Nagahama Castle to the north, Omizo Castle on the opposite side of the lake, and Sakamoto Castle nearer to Kyoto. After Oda's death, Hashiba (Toyotomi) Hideyoshi applied this same strategy and had his nephew Hidetsugu build a castle in Omihachiman with canals that connected to Lake Biwa through the marshes.

琵琶湖の城郭ネットワーク
Castles on Lake Biwa

織田信長の甥・信澄の大溝城
Omizo Castle was built by Oda Nobunaga's nephew, Nobuzumi.

比叡山延暦寺焼き討ち後、織田信長が明智光秀に築かせた坂本城
Sakamoto Castle was built by Akechi Mitsuhide at the behest of Oda Nobunaga after burning down parts of Enryakuji Temple on Mt. Hiei.

安土城焼失後、秀吉が秀次に築かせた八幡山城
Hachimanyama Castle built by Toyotomi Hidetsugu at the behest of his uncle Toyotomi Hideyoshi, after Azuchi Castle was burned down.

長浜城

羽柴（豊臣）秀吉の出世城として知られる長浜城（写真は太閤井戸跡）
Nagahama Castle is known historically as a step-up for Hashiba (Toyotomi) Hideyoshi. (The photo is of the site where the Taiko well had been.)

佐和山城

石田三成の居城として知られる佐和山城
Sawayama Castle is best known for being the residence of Ishida Mitsunari.

安土城天主付近
Revetment of the main tower of Azuchi Castle

三、水運を重視した武将たち

大溝城 Omizo Castle

　安土城の対岸に信長の甥・信澄が大溝城を築城。琵琶湖の内湖である乙女ヶ池に突出させた方形の本丸を中心に、湖に面して二の丸、三の丸があり、すべての堀が湖と直結していた。（高島市勝野）

Oda Nobunaga's nephew, Nobuzumi, built Omizo Castle on the opposite side of Lake Biwa from his uncle's castle in Azuchi. The citadel jutted out into Lake Otomegaike, just inland from Lake Biwa, and was flanked by auxiliary baileys that faced the water. All of the moats connected to the lake. (Katsuno, Takashima City)

高島市勝野に立つ万葉歌碑
Monument to the Man'yo Verses in Katsuno, Takashima City

良港としてにぎわった勝野津の浜
Katsunotsu was once a bustling port.

大溝城天守台跡
Former site where the main tower of Omizo Castle stood

三、水運を重視した武将たち

分部家旧城下町
The Castle Town of the Wakebe Clan

　大溝城跡と旧城下町地域は、分部氏による街並み整備が行われ、山や井戸から自噴する古式水道や水路は今も住民に利用されている。

The streetscape of the town around Omizo Castle was reorganized by the Wakebe Clan. The original aqueducts and canals that flowed naturally from the mountains and wells are still being used by residents today.

城下町の面影を伝える「惣門」跡
The Somon Gate gives you an idea of what the castle town looked like long ago.

毎年5月には曳山が繰り出し豪勢な大溝祭が開催される
In May every year, colorful floats are rolled out for the popular Omizomatsuri Festival.

旧城下町の背割り水路（高島市勝野）
Aqueduct running down the middle of the street of the former castle town (Katsuno, Takashima City)

街道沿いではふなずしや、酢、酒など発酵食品製造業が盛ん
Along the road are found many businesses that make fermented foods like Funazushi, vinegar and sake.

今も使われる古式水道
The original water system is still being used today.

三、水運を重視した武将たち

天下布武の安土城 Azuchi Castle in the Unification of Japan

　安土城は織田信長による天下統一事業「天下布武」のシンボルとして築かれたが、本能寺の変後まもなく焼失した。(近江八幡市安土町)
Oda Nobunaga built Azuchi Castle as a symbol of his "Tenkafubu" strategy to unify Japan, but it was lost to fire shortly after Oda was forced to commit suicide by his own General Akechi Mitsuhide.

信長一周忌に秀吉が築いた信長廟所
Mausoleum built by Toyotomi Hideyoshi to honor Oda Nobunaga

信長が築城した安土山と右に広がる繖山
Arial view of Oda's Azuchi Castle and Mt. Kinugasa to the right

天主に続く大手道
Approach to the castle keep

発掘された安土城の金箔瓦
Gold leaf rooftile from Azuchi Castle

安土城復元想像模型
Model of Azuchi Castle

三、水運を重視した武将たち

水運を生かした安土城と城下町
Marine Transportation In and Around Azuchi Castle and Town

琵琶湖のそばに築城された安土城には、湖上交通の利便性を背景にした、東西文化の交流についての大きな成果が見られる。

Building Azuchi Castle on Lake Biwa boosted cultural exchange between eastern and western Japan because of the benefits of marine transportation.

安土城から西の湖を望む。城の周りは内湖が巡る
Lake Nishinoko seen from Azuchi Castle. This inland lake wrapped around the castle.

信長が優遇したキリスト教学校（セミナリヨ）跡
Site of a Christian seminary that received special treatment from Nobunaga

「東の宮さん」と呼ばれ信仰を集める新宮神社の拝殿
Worship hall at Shingujinja Shrine known to many as "Higashinomiya-san (East shrine)"

セミナリヨ跡は水際にあり、安土城の堀に通じている
The former seminary was on the water and connected to the castle by canals.

常楽寺港は西の湖を介して琵琶湖につながっている
The port in Jorakuji was connected to Lake Biwa through Lake Nishinoko.

三、水運を重視した武将たち

伊庭内湖 Inland Lake Iba

近江源氏佐々木氏の一族の伊庭氏は、領主の六角氏と肩を並べるほどの勢力をもっていたといい、その拠点は伊庭千軒といわれるほど繁栄した。集落内の伊庭城跡には、西行や芭蕉とともに三大放浪歌人といわれる宗祇の句碑が立つ。(東近江市伊庭町)

The Iba Family were a branch of the Omi-Genji and Sasaki Clans, and reportedly wielded as much influence and power as the Rokkaku Clan that ruled over parts of Omi Province. The territory where they lived and worked was so prosperous that it was described as a "community of 1,000 homes". At the site where the family castle once stood, there is a monument to Iio Sogi (1421 – 1502) who is considered one of Japan's three great roaming poets alongside Hoshi Saigyo (1118 – 1190) and Matsuo Basho (1644 - 1694). (Ibacho, Higashiomi City)

伊庭内湖から繖山を望む
Mt. Kinugasa seen from Inland Lake Iba

直径13mの大水車は伊庭内湖のシンボル。アウトドアスポーツのスポットとして人気が高い
Measuring 13 m across, this waterwheel is the symbol of Inland Lake Iba. The lake is a popular spot for outdoor activities.

浄土真宗本願寺派の妙楽寺門内には4ヶ寺が集合。集落の中心に位置し景観を特徴づけている。
Inside the gate to Myorakuji Temple are four temples of the Jodoshinshu-Honganji Sect of Buddhism. The sanctuary is found at the center of the village and adds a distinctive tone to the streetscape.

伊庭の集落に恵みを与える繖山。(写真中央)
Mt. Kinugasa (center) brings the best of nature's blessings to the village of Iba.

水路が走る伊庭の暮らしと信仰
Canals Amidst Life and Faith in Iba

　繖山に発する瓜生川の流れが集落内に引き込まれ、水路として網の目のように張り巡らされている。地元では「カワ」と呼ばれる水路が、外からの財を伊庭にもたらした。

The waters of the Uryu River that originates on Mt. Kinugasa have been channeled and spread throughout the village via a network of canals. Locally looked at rivers, these canals historically brought outside wealth to Iba.

随所にみられるカワト（川戸）
Known as a kawato (literally "door to the river"), access points to the canals are found all across the village.

カワに設けられている生簀
Fish pen in a canal

2001年、宗祇500年祭の時に城跡に建てられた宗祇の句碑「かげすずし山に重なる軒の松」
This monument to the poet Iio Sogi was erected on the former site of Iba Castle in 2001, as part of celebrations marking the poet's 500th birthday. The inscription is from a haiku of his and roughly translates as "Many pine trees on the mountain give cool shade".

本殿から500m、断崖絶壁のある山道を3基の神輿が勇壮に引き下ろされる「伊庭の坂下し祭」
One of three portable Shinto alters being carried down a steep rugged 500 m trail from Sanposanjinja Shrine during the Iba Sakakudashi Festival.

祭り当日の大濱神社仁王堂。鎌倉時代の創建
Niodo Temple (Ohamajinja Shrine) on the day of the Iba Sakakudashi Festival. The temple was built in the Kamakura Period (1185 - 1333).

四、近江商人を生んだ水環境

4. A Water Environment That Spurred Trade in Omi

織田信長が舟遊びに興じたと伝わる安土から近江八幡に広がる八幡堀（近江八幡市新町）。西の湖に続くこの堀は、羽柴（豊臣）秀次によって開削され、物資の運搬に大きく貢献した。

Oda Nobunaga reportedly enjoyed boating on the Hachimanbori Canal between Azuchi and Omihachiman. The canal was dug by Hashiba (Toyotomi) Hidetsugu and, because it connected to Lake Nishinoko, it contributed greatly to the transportation of goods.

春の芽だちを促すために焼かれる西の湖のヨシ原（近江八幡市）
Reeds along Lake Nishinoko are set afire to promote budding in spring. (Omihashiman City)

西の湖 Lake Nishinoko

刈り取ったヨシは円形に立てて干す
Cut reeds are bundled and stood in a circle to dry.

かつては足で水車をこぎ田に水を送った（体験イベントでのようす）
A long time ago, waterwheels were driven by manpower to irrigate rice paddies. (This photo was taken at a special event for experiencing life long ago.)

新緑のヨシ原を手漕ぎ遊覧船が行く。ヨシキリの鳴き声が聞こえるのどかな情景
Sightseeing cruises row visitors through the fresh green marshes.

四、近江商人を生んだ水環境

秀次のまちづくりと八幡商人の誕生
Town Development by Toyotomi Hidetsugu and Birth of the Omi Merchants

　八幡山での築城に着手した羽柴（豊臣）秀次は、琵琶湖と城下町を結ぶ運河を開くとともに、碁盤の目状のまちづくりを進めた。しかし不運にも短い生涯を終え、八幡山城は廃城となり、徳川の世には天領となった。その後、この地から江戸へ、北海道へと商圏を広げた八幡商人が誕生する。

Soon after he started building a castle on Mt. Hachiman, Hashiba (Toyotomi) Hidetsugu had the castle town developed like a grid and dug canals to link it to Lake Biwa. However, infighting within his family led to Hidetsugu's early death and what had been constructed for his castle was torn down, paving the way for Ieyasu Tokugawa's rule over the area. Still, the canals he built later gave birth to a clever group of merchants who took their business in Omi to Tokyo and Hokkaido.

八幡公園に立つ秀次像
Statue of Hashiba (Toyotomi) Hidetsugu in Hachiman Park.

本家を近江に残した豪商の商家が連なる新町通り。
その奥が八幡山
Greatly successful merchants built their homes/businesses along Shinmachidori. Mt. Hachiman can be seen in the background.

琵琶湖に通じる八幡堀は物資の運搬などで町の発展に大きく寄与し、現在は県内有数の観光地として活況をみせる
Because it connected to Lake Biwa, the Hachimanbori Canal greatly contributed to the town's development through the transportation of goods, etc. Today, it is one of the most popular tourist destinations in Shiga Prefecture.

写真提供：近江商人博物館
Photo courtesy of the Omi Merchant Museum

近江商人ゆかりの五個荘金堂
Gokashokondocho and the Omi Merchants

　江戸時代後期から活躍した五個荘商人の屋敷は、東近江市五個荘金堂町を中心に多く残り、水を生活の中に取り込んだ暮らしぶりを伝える。屋敷内には連通管で井戸から風呂に水を引く先進的な仕掛けがある。

Many of the homes belonging to local merchants who were active in the late Edo Period (18th – 19th century) can be found today in and around Gokashokondocho, Higashiomi City. It is evident from the architecture and streetscape just how much "water" was an integral part of life back in the day. Advanced for the time, piping carried water from wells to bathtubs inside the homes.

外村宇兵衛邸（近江商人屋敷）のカワト（川戸）
Water access point, known as a kawato, on the property of the merchant Tonomura Uhee

五個荘金堂の川中地蔵
Jizo alter in the canal in Gokashokondocho

明治期に活躍した藤井善助邸（近江商人屋敷）の庭園は琵琶湖をかたどる池が中心
The garden of Fujii Zensuke, a local merchant of the Meiji Period (1868 – 1912), has a pond modeled after Lake Biwa at its center.

質素倹約が生活信条の商家
A Frugal Way of Living and Doing Business in Omi

　近江から生まれた商人は地域によりそれぞれ特性があるが、いずれも自分の利益を求める前に、相手のためになる商いを心がけた。これが今「三方（さんぽう）よし」の理念として広く知られる。また、「普段の生活は質素に必要なものは惜しみなく」が彼らの信条である。

Though there were regional differences amongst the merchants from Omi, one thing they all had in common was to gear business to the benefit of the other party before pursuing personal gains. The policy is known today as "Sanpoyoshi" (basically meaning "to the benefit of the buyer, seller and community"). They also lived frugally by "spending money only on the necessities of daily life".

「筏」三部作で著名な作家・外村繁の生家の井戸
Well found on the property where Tonomura Shigeru, author of the popular trilogy "Ikada", was born,

四、近江商人を生んだ水環境　77

五、湖畔に生きる

5. Living Lakeside

琵琶湖の恵みを享受しながらも自然との闘いの中で暮らす水辺の人々。永年の生活の知恵や、先人が築き上げた歴史や文化の中で、昔も今も変わらぬ時間が経過している。

Lake Biwa has many blessing to give, but living along her shores is nonetheless a battle with nature's ways. The environment has shaped a way of life, culture and history in which, today, time passes slowly just like long ago.

高島市マキノ町の海津浜に残る桟橋の跡
Remains of a pier off Kaizuhama Beach in Makinocho, Takashima City

高島市海津・西浜・知内の水辺景観
Waterfront Landscape in Kaizu, Nishihama and Chinai, Takashima City

　かつて、港町・宿場町として栄えた琵琶湖北西部のこの地域は、湖岸に築かれた防波石垣のある特徴的な景観として2008年、重要文化的景観に選定された。

A long time ago, the northwestern corner of Lake Biwa prospered as a port and layover post along Japan's old roads. The characteristic landscape of stone breakwaters built along the shoreline was selected an Important Cultural Landscape in 2008.

湖岸に連綿と続く石垣は、大波大風に崩れる湖岸の家々を見た代官・西与一左衛門によって築かれた
The stone walls that run in an unbroken line along the shore were built by the governor of the Kofu Domain, Nishi Yoichizaemon after seeing numerous homes along the shore destroyed by waves and winds.

街道沿いの酒蔵
Sake brewery

野菜などを洗う橋板。琵琶湖の水は生活の中に息づいている
Used for washing vegetables, this plank shows just how much a part of life Lake Biwa is for people living near its shores.

水が湧き出るところに「イケ」を掘り、分け合いながら使う暮らしが続く
It is still common practice to dig ponds where spring water is found, and share water resources.

五、湖畔に生きる　81

●古写真に見る湖畔の人々の暮らし
Old Photos of Life Along the Shores of Lake Biwa

写真提供:高島市　Photos courtesy of Takashima City

住民そろって地引網を曳く
Residents pulling a seine

祭礼の日の少年たち
Children on the day of a festival

湖辺の人々の暮らし
Women washing vegetables in the lake

高島市針江・霜降の水辺景観
Water's Edge in Harie and Shimofuri, Takashima City

「カバタ」（川端）から湧き出た湧水（生水）は針江大川から内湖にそそぐ。湖岸にはヨシ原が広がり、日本の原風景といえる景観が残る。ヨシ原は琵琶湖に棲む多様な魚類の産卵場所となり、静かな郷に生きた水が巡る貴重な景観を見せる。

Spring water that makes its way into the Harieokawa River flows into inland lakes. Reeds grow along the banks and provide a variety of lake fish a place to spawn and lay their eggs. Water is at the core of a delicate ecosystem, an unspoiled landscape and a peaceful lifestyle in the countryside.

針江の漁場を大切にした漁師・田中三五郎さんは、今森光彦さんの写真の被写体となった
Tanaka Sangoro was a fisherman who cared for the fishing grounds in Harie. His legacy is the focal point of this photo by Imamori Mitsuhiko.

五、湖畔に生きる

高島市新旭町針江では安曇川の伏流水と比良山系からの地下水を起源とする湧水が集落各所に自噴し、これらを飲料水や生活水として利用するカバタが現在の暮らしにも生き、エコな水循環システムが形成されている。

Water seeped from the riverbed along the Ado River and groundwater from the Hira Mountains resurface as spring water in the Harie area of Shin'asahicho, Takashima City. Still today, this spring water is accessed for drinking and other daily uses by way of a time-honored ecological system known as a kabata.

集落内を流れる針江大川。定期的に住民が川底清掃を行い、琵琶湖にきれいな水を返す努力を惜しまない。カバタには様々なお札が張られ、「川中地蔵」には水への感謝が祈りの形として表われている
The Harieokawa River flows through the village. Residents periodically clean the riverbed to make sure the water returning to Lake Biwa is clean. Their gratitude for the blessings nature provides is further expressed by posting messages on kabatas and praying before a Jizo statue placed in the river.

飲料水はモトイケから汲んで使う
Drinking water is drawn from aquifers known as motoike.

カバタは、水が湧き出るモトイケと、ここから流れる水を受けるツボイケ、さらに外のハヤイケで構成される
This kabata consists of a motoike (aquifer) from which water springs, a tsuboike (spillover) that pools the spring water, and a hayaike (cistern) outside of that.

五、湖畔に生きる　87

中世の歴史文化が息づく
湖畔の集落・菅浦

A Gem of Medieval History and Culture on the Shores of Lake Biwa, Sugaura

　長浜市西浅井町菅浦の須賀神社に伝わる膨大な「菅浦文書」は、この地が先進的な自治共同体であり、人々が船を使い、琵琶湖一円のまち・むらと活発な交流を重ねてきたことを教えてくれる。

Housed under lock and key at Sugajinja Shrine in the Sugaura area of Nishiazaicho, Nagahama City, the massive collection of historical records known as the "Sugaura Archives" tell of a forward-looking, self-governing community that navigated Lake Biwa to actively trade with the towns and hamlets along its shores.

ヤンマーの農村工場が点在する菅浦の集落
Small factories of Yanmar dot the idyllic village landscape in Sugaura.

中世以降、琵琶湖で活躍した丸子船
Known as a marukobune, wooden boats such as this were used on Lake Biwa between the 12th and 18th centuries.

湖に張り付くような菅浦の集落
Village of Sugaura hugging the shoreline on Lake Biwa

橋板を使う暮らしは当たり前に息づいている
Washing vegetables in the lake is an everyday routine.

かつては集落の四方に存在していた四足門が、現在も東西の2ヶ所に残る。集落への出入りの検察を行っていたと考えられる
A long time ago, gates supported by four pillars existed on all sides of the village. Today, two remain, one each to the east and west. They most likely served as checkpoints for entering and leaving the village.

須賀神社から琵琶湖を望む。拝殿前の石階段に「素足で参詣すること」という注意書きがある
Lake Biwa seen from Sugajinja Shrine. A notice at the foot of the stone steps heading to the hall of worship reminds those coming to pray to "remove their shoes".

沖島に住む Living on Okishima Island

　琵琶湖最大の島・沖島（近江八幡市沖島町）には300名余りが暮らす。人が住む湖中の島は世界的にも珍しく、日本では唯一。
　平安時代、保元・平治の乱に敗れた清和源氏の流れをくむ人が住み着いたと伝わる。戦国時代には水運を重視した織田信長に加勢したことにより、その後500年以上にわたって対岸周辺の漁場権利を得た。

Some 300 people live year-round on Lake Biwa's largest island, Okishima (Okishimacho, Omihachiman City). It is rare to find people living on an island in a lake anywhere in the world and Okishima is the only such place in Japan.

The first people to settle on the island are believed to have been descendants of the Seiwa Genji Clan after their defeat in the Hogen (1156) and Heiji Wars (1159). During Japan's Age of Civil Wars (1467 – 1590), they were awarded rights to the fishing grounds off their shores by Oda Nobunaga, who understood the importance of over-water transportation, for the support they showed him. They retained those rights for over 500 years.

沖島港近くに民家が密集している
Homes concentrate in the area around the port.

現在は畑となっている採石場跡
A former quarry is used for farming today.

島には自動車がないので自転車が唯一の移動手段。時間がゆっくりと流れる
There are no cars on the island, so bicycles are the sole means for getting around. That is one of the reasons why time passes slowly.

島で行われる左義長の飾り物
The first full moon of the new year is celebrated on the island with colorful decorations.

● 琵琶湖八珍 8 Gastronomic Delicacies from Lake Biwa

　日本最大、最古の琵琶湖には54種の固有種が生息する。豊かな自然の恵みは貴重な食材として長い歴史の中で親しまれてきた。それらを含む特徴的な魚介類の中から、ビワマス・ニゴロブナ・ホンモロコ・イサザ・ゴリ（ウロリ・ヨシノボリ）・コアユ・スジエビ・ハスの8種が「琵琶湖八珍」として選定された。

コアユの天ぷら
Koayu tempura

モロコの素焼き
Grilled moroko

ハスの塩焼き
Grilled hasu with salt

As Japan's largest and oldest lake, Biwako is a habitat for 54 indigenous species of fish and crustaceans, many of which have long been prized for their gastronomic value. Eight of them have been selected as delicacies – Biwa trout, nigorobuna, honmoroko, isaza, biwa yoshinobori, koayu, suji-ebi and hasu.

ニゴロブナの発酵食品ふなずし
Funazushi (Fermented nigorobuna)

ハス(左)とエビ豆(スジエビと大豆の炊き合わせ)
Grilled hasu (left) and suji-ebi (right) with soybean past rub

ビワマスの造り
Raw biwa trout

沖島の夕景
Sunset over Okishima Island

六、水系に暮らす

6. Life Along Lake Biwa's Feeder Rivers

太鼓や鉦を鳴らして祭りの準備が整ったことを知らせる
Drums and gongs are used to announce that festival preparations have been made.

高時川水系 Takatoki River

長浜市高月町持寺・尾山の野神祭は、自然の豊かさや水の恵みに感謝すると同時に、水争いをなくすという意味も含まれていた。目の前に大きな湖があるにもかかわらず高時川の水に頼っていた農民の暮らしの中から生まれた信仰の形で、地域によって様々な形で行われる。

当人は御幣を注連縄に結わえる
This man is about to tie the staff with pleated streamers he is holding to the straw festoon wrapped around the tree.

長浜市余呉町菅並での冬準備作業
Preparing for winter in the Suganami area of Yogocho, Nagahama City

Shinto rituals are performed in the Mochidera and Oyama areas of Takatsukicho, Nagahama City to thank Mother Nature for the plentiful blessings she yields and to eliminate quarreling over water distribution. Despite the mammoth lake right before their eyes, farming communities that depended on the Takatoki River developed their own system of beliefs. These rituals vary in format by location.

長浜市余呉町菅並の観音堂。観音像の多くが地域の人々によって守られている
Kannondo Temple in the Suganami area of Yogocho, Nagahama City. The many Kannon statues are cared for by local residents.

姉川水系 Ane River

　伊吹山地を源流とする姉川沿いの東草野地区（米原市甲津原・曲谷・甲賀・吉槻）は関西屈指の豪雪地帯である。ここには、伝統的な生活文化と密接に結びついたカワト、イケ、ショウズ、サワという呼び名の水利用の姿を見ることができる。1953年には旧井堰19ヶ所を統合し、維持管理の節減や分水の合理化を図るための姉川合同井堰が建設された。

Some of the heaviest snowfall in the Kansai is seen in the Higashikusano area (Kozuhara, Magatani, Koga and Yoshitsuki, Maibara City) along the Ane River that originates in the Ibuki Mountains. Here, you can see traditional ways of water usage that are inseparably tied to the local lifestyle and culture – kawato (an aqueduct dammed up with a board), ike (pond), shozu (crystal stream) and sawa (washbasin). In 1953, 19 former dams were replaced with a single larger dam to reduce maintenance work and rationally distribute water.

合同井堰から分水されている小田分水
Water diversion in Yanaida

小田扇状分水と伊吹山　Kodani Fan Diversion with Mt. Ibuki in the background

国の重要文化的景観に選定された長浜市東草野曲谷集落の全景
Arial view of Magadani Village in Higashikusano, Nagahama City. The village was selected an Important Cultural Landscape of Japan.

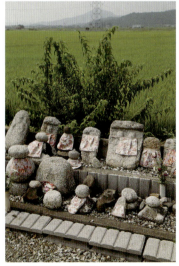

姉川古戦場近くの地蔵
Jizo statues near the Anegawa Battlefield

1870年6月、織田信長は近江に侵攻し、姉川を挟んで浅井長政と対峙する。戦の3年後に小谷城は落城し、浅井家は滅亡した。当時の合戦のすさまじさを語る「血原」の地名が残り、戦死者の慰霊碑などが立つ。

In June 1570, Oda Nobunaga invaded Omi and confronted Azai Nagamasa at the Ane River. After three years of fighting, Odani Castle fell and the Azai Family was killed off. A memorial to those who died in battle stands in a location interestingly named Chihara (literally "field of blood"), which accurately sums up what the battle was like.

●雨乞い御礼の太鼓踊り・Rain Dancing to the Beat of Drums

米原市井之口の太鼓踊り　Drumming and dancing in Inokuchi, Maibara City

米原市春照の太鼓踊り
Drumming and dancing in Suijo, Maibara City

水利の悪い扇状地で暮らす人々は、水源である伊吹山に対し、祈りと感謝の気持ちが強く、山麓9ヶ所で雨乞い御礼の太鼓踊りが山に向かって奉納される。朝日豊年太鼓踊りは1300年前、この地が開かれた当時から続く素朴な民衆芸能で、国選択無形文化財に指定されている。

Because of the poor water supply, people living in this alluvial fan harbor tremendous respect and appreciation for Mt. Ibuki as it serves as their watershed. In 9 places at the foot of the mountain, this reverence is demonstrated by rain dances to the beat of drums. Ever since it was first performed 1300 years ago, Asahihonentaikoodori has been continued in this area as a rustic form of folk entertainment. It is today a designated Intangible Cultural Property of Japan.

滋賀県下に広がる太鼓踊り。写真は犬上郡甲良町北落のおはな踊り
Drumming and dancing events span Shiga Prefecture. This photo captures a moment during Ohanaodori in the Kitaochi area of Koracho, Inukamigun.

御池川上流域の政所は茶の産地として知られる（東近江市政所町）
Located in the upper reaches of the Oike River, Mandokoro is known as a tea growing area. (Mandokorocho, Higashiomi City)

愛知川水系 Echi River

鈴鹿山脈を源流とする愛知川は、杠葉尾で神崎川と合流し、湖東平野に入ると蛇行して琵琶湖に至る。上流の奥永源寺地区には惟高親王伝説が残り、全国に良材を求めた木地師たちは政所茶を全国に広めたという。

The Echi River that originates in the Suzuka Mountain Range merges with the Kanzaki River at Yuzurio, then snakes its way across the plains east of Lake Biwa before emptying into the lake. In the Okueigenji area at the river's upper reaches, legend has it that the Prince Koretaka (844 - 897) taught craftsmen how to turn wood on a lathe. Then, seeking good quality wood to work with, these craftsmen fanned out across the country, bringing tea produced in Mandokoro with them and thus making it known throughout Japan.

ろくろ製法を伝えたとされる惟高親王の墓所（東近江市君ヶ畑町）
Tomb of the Prince Koretaka, the purported founder of woodturning in Japan. (Kimigahatacho, Higashiomi City)

全国の木地師が信仰する大皇器地祖神社（東近江市君ヶ畑町）のお札
Talisman given out by Okimikijisojinja (Kimigahatacho, Higashiomi City). The shrine is revered by woodworkers all across the country.

●紅葉を競い合う名刹
• Temples Known for Their Autumnal Foliage

永源寺（東近江市永源寺高野町）
鎌倉時代、寂室元光和尚が伽藍を建立したことに始まり、その後、佐々木氏の庇護のもと多くの学僧が集まり栄えた。
Eigenji (Eigenjitakanocho, Higashiomi City)
Eigenji began when the Priest Jakushitsu Genko (1290 – 1367) built a large temple. It later flourished as a monastery with the protection of the Sasaki Clan.

西明寺（犬上郡甲良町池寺）
平安時代仁明天皇の勅願で三修上人が開山。鎌倉時代の建築である三重塔は国宝で、内部には極彩色の金剛界など極楽浄土が描かれている。
Saimyoji (Ikedera, Koracho, Inukamigun)
Saimyoji was built by the Priest Sanshu (829 – 899) at the behest of the Heian Emperor Nimmyo (810 – 850). The three-tier pagoda built in the Kamakura Period (1185 - 1333) is a National Treasure and has ornately colored murals depicting the Diamond Realm and other features of the Buddhist Land of Pure Bliss.

金剛輪寺（愛知郡愛荘町松尾寺）
聖武天皇の勅願で行基が開いた天台の巨刹。本堂の大悲閣が国宝のほか多くの重要文化財を有し、桃山時代の茶室「水雲閣」を中心とした庭園は趣がある。
Kongorinji (Matsuoji, Aishocho, Echigun)
This large temple of the Tendai Sect was built by the Priest Gyoki (668 – 749) at the behest of the Emperor Shomu (701 – 756). It has numerous Important Cultural Properties, most noteworthy of which is the main hall that houses the Kannon. The garden with its "Suiunkaku" tea arbor from the Momoyama Period (1568 - 1600) is also spectacular.

百済寺（東近江市百済寺町）
聖徳太子の発願で造られ、本尊の「植木観音」は秘仏。鈴鹿山脈を借景にした池泉回遊式庭園は、自然の谷や川を表わす。
Hyakusaiji (Hyakusaijicho, Higashiomi City)
Normally kept from public viewing, the wooden statue known as the "Shokkikannon" that the temple venerates was made at the request of Prince Shotoku (574 – 622). The garden is set against the Suzuka Mountain Range and landscaped to represent a valley and river. It applies the classical design of footpaths around a central pond.

湖東平野を流れる愛知川
Echi River snaking its way across the plains east of Lake Biwa

河川敷に自然石の地蔵が作られる
Jizo alter assembled with natural stones in a riverbed

　愛知川中流域の東近江市青山では、河川敷に斎場を作り、宗派に関係なくお盆のお精霊迎えを地域全員で行う。川が冥界と現界の結界と考えられているのであろうか。

At its midreaches, the Echi River passes through Aoyama, Higashiomi City. There, everyone from the local area makes alters in the riverbed to welcome the spirits, regardless of denomination, during the Obon season. The river is thought of as a portal between the underworld and the real world.

愛知川河川敷で行われる東近江市青山のお精霊迎え
The people of Aoyama, Higashiomi City welcome spirits during the Obon season by building alters in the riverbed of the Echi River.

お精霊迎えの参加を村人に呼び掛ける子どもたち
Children calling residents to take part in welcoming the spirits

六、水系に暮らす

野洲川から近江富士とよばれる三上山を望む
Mt. Mikami, referred to by some as "Omi's Mt. Fuji," seen from the Yasu River.

かつて名所と知られた赤岩付近。野洲川流域からはゾウの足跡化石が多く見られる
This area near Akaiwa is reputed for its historical importance, as many fossilized elephant footprints have been found in the river basin.

野洲川流域 Yasu River Basin

　三重県との県境の御在所岳を水源とする野洲川は、主流延長61kmの県内有数の大河で「近江太郎」と呼ばれる。たびたび水害に見舞われ、水利の争いが繰り返されたが、わが国最大級の放水路新設は、人々に安らかな生活をもたらした。

Nicknamed "Omitaro", the Yasu River is amongst the largest rivers in Shiga Prefecture as its main course stretches 61 km from its origin on Mt. Gozaisho along the border with Mie Prefecture. From time to time, the river had overflowed its banks and was repeatedly at the center of water disputes, so a spillway of the largest class in Japan was built and brought some peace of mind to those living on the river.

野洲川下流域での生物調査
Wildlife survey in the lower reaches of the Yasu River

野洲には18世紀中ごろ130軒の晒し屋があり、野洲川の伏流水で白く晒して商品価値を高めた近江麻布は、近江商人によって全国に広まった（「近江名所図会」より）
Around the mid 18th century, there were about 130 bleaching huts in the Yasu River. Bleaching the locally produced hemp cloth white in the infiltrating water increased its value. Omi merchants sold the products all across Japan. (Source: "Omi Meisho Zue")

安曇川流域 Ado River Basin

　安曇川は、丹波高地の百井峠（京都市）に水源をもち、大津市葛川地区を経て、高島市内を南北に走り琵琶湖にそそぐ。上流域には、奈良や京の都に建築用材を伐りだした杣山が広がる。

The Ado Rivers originates from Momoi
Pass in the Tanba Highlands (Kyoto City). It then crosses the Katsuragawa area of Otsu City and runs through Takashima City from the south to the north, before pouring into Lake Biwa. The upper reaches are nestled in timberland that was lumbered into building materials used in Nara and Kyoto when these cities were the capital.

安曇川上流の思古淵付近。かつて筏流しが盛んに行われていた渓谷
Near Shikofuchi in the upper reaches of the Ado River. Long ago, floating timber through this valley was a bustling trade.

安曇川下流域で行われる琵琶湖の伝統的な簗漁
Traditional fishing technique from Lake Biwa using a weir in the lower reaches of the Ado River.

高島市今津町保坂では、若狭街道(京都〜小浜)と九里半街道(今津〜小浜)が分岐・合流する
In the Hozaka area of Imazucho, Takashima City, the Wakasakaido (Kyoto – Obama) and Kurihankaido (Imazu – Obama) split and merge.

高島市朽木古屋の盆行事では、安曇川源流の一つ針畑川に自然石の地蔵が作られる
For Obon in Kutsukifuruya, Takashima City, Jizo alters are made with river stones in the Harihata River. It is one of the sources of the Ado River.

高島市朽木小川の思子淵神社の御神木ヒノキ
Sacred cypress tree at Shikobuchijinja Shrine in Kutsukikogawa, Takashima City

大津市葛川梅ノ木町の志子渕神社
Shikobuchijinja Shrine in Katsuragawaumenokicho, Otsu City

シコブチ信仰 Protected by Shikobuchi

　杣山で切り出した木材を水上輸送する筏乗りや、安曇川水系に暮らす人々は、川の魔物から守ってくれる「シコブチ神」を信仰している。その祠や社の分布は安曇川流域とその源流に限られており、いずれも川を見渡せる場所にある。

The people that lived along the Ado River and floated felled lumber downriver from the timberland prayed to a deity known as "Shikobuchi" to protect them from river demons. The shrines for that and their smaller versions called hokora are found only in the Ado River basin and headwaters, and, in all cases, are placed in locations from where the river can be seen.

高島市安曇川町中野の思子淵神社
Shikobuchijinja Shrine in Nakano, Adogawacho, Takashima City

大津市葛川坊村町の志古淵神社
Shikobuchijinja Shrine in Katsuragawabomuracho, Otsu City

高島市朽木小川の思子淵神社
Shikobuchijinja Shrine in Kutsukikogawa, Takashima City

醒井宿 Samegaishuku

　中山道61番目の宿場・醒井宿（米原市醒井）は、山からの湧水を水源とする地蔵川に沿う。水中花のバイカモ（梅花藻）がゆらめきハリヨが泳ぐ清流の周辺には、多くの伝説が残り、古くからの歴史を伝えている。

Samegai in Maibara City was the 61st layover post on the Nakasendo Road. It is located on the Jizo River that originates from a mountain spring. Nearby streams are home to indigenous species of aquatic crowfoot and stickleback. The area has a long history and is tied to numerous legends.

醒井木彫美術館。当地出身の森大造の作品のほか、地元彫刻師の作品を多く所蔵
Samegai Woodcarving Museum. The collection includes works by Mori Taizo and other local artists.

地蔵川のバイカモ（梅花藻）
Indigenous species of aquatic crowfoot in the Jizo River

８月の地蔵盆には「つくりもん」の展示で賑わう
The town puts craftworks on display during the Jizobon season in August.

旧問屋場跡を復元し、醒井宿史料館として開放している
This former livery stable/supply depot was renovated and opened as the Samegaishuku Museum.

地蔵川の清流に泳ぐ魚たち
Fish swimming in the pristine waters of the Jizo River

醒井の三名水の一つ「十王水」
Juosui, one of three prized water resources in Samegai.

西行が飲み残した茶の泡で子を宿した娘の伝説が残る「西行水」
Saigyosui. Legend has it that a young maiden working at a tea shop became pregnant after drinking the tea left by the poet Hoshi Saigyo.

居醒の清水などから湧き出る水が地蔵川を満たす
Spring water like that coming from Isame feeds the Jizo River.

●滋賀の名水 • Prized Water Sources in Shiga

居醒の清水（米原市醒井）
ヤマトタケルノミコトの傷を癒したと伝わる
Isamenoshimizu (Samegai, Maibara City)
The water from this source is said to have healed the wounds of the legendary prince Yamato Takeru.

堂来清水（長浜市高山町）
三国峠の夜叉ケ池を姉池とし、榧谷山腹の妹池に発すると伝わる堂来清水。神事の洗米水としても生かされている。
Doraishozu (Takayamacho, Nagahama City)
Doraishozu is said to originate from Lake Imoto on Mt. Kayatani. It is used in Shinto rituals to wash rice.

十王村の水（彦根市西今町）
『淡海木間攫』などにも記され、地元では「母乳の地蔵尊」として信仰され、地蔵堂が大切に守られている。
Juomuranomizu (Nishiimacho, Hikone City)
This prized water source appears in the "Omikomazarae" registry of towns, shrines and temples. It is cared for by Jizodo Temple and the local community worships it as the "Guardian Deity of Breast Feeding".

泉神社湧水（米原市大清水）
日本の名水百選の一つ。天智天皇の時代、弓馬操練の場所でそれに関わる人が住んでいたところと伝わる。

Izumijinjawakimizu (Oshimizu, Maibara City)
Selected one of Japan's 100 Best Water Sources, the site where this spring water emerges is believed to have hosted lodgings for a facility where people trained in archery and horsemanship in the time of the Emperor Tenji (626 – 672).

走井（大津市大谷町）
国道1号沿いの月心寺内にある。歌川広重の東海道五十三次にも描かれ、古くから旅人の喉を潤してきた。

Hashirii (Otanicho, Otsu City)
This well is located on the grounds of Gesshinji Temple, which sits just off of Nat. Rt. 1. The artist Utagawa Hiroshige depicted it in "Otsujuku in the 1830s" of his "53 Stations of the Tokaido" series, testifying to the well's history of quenching the thirst of travelers since long ago.

六、水系に暮らす

七、琵琶湖の源流

7. Headwaters

神崎川上流
Upper reaches of the Kanzaki River

高時川上流のザゼンソウ
Skunk cabbage in the upper reaches of the Takatoki River

琵琶湖の水源 Origin

　日本のほぼ中央に位置する琵琶湖は、四方を山に囲まれた滋賀県の人々の暮らしに大きな影響を与えてきた。県内を流れる川は琵琶湖にそそぎ、やがて瀬田川などを経て、淀川、大阪湾から太平洋へと続く。長い水の旅の源が琵琶湖を取り巻く山々にある。

Lake Biwa is located roughly in the middle of Japan and surrounded by mountains on all sides. These mountains are where the waters of Lake Biwa begin a long journey that starts with the feeder rivers emptying into the lake and ultimately, via the Seta and other rivers, continues on to the Yodo River, Osaka Bay and the Pacific Ocean.

犬上川源流　Headwaters of the Inukami River

神崎川上流。流れをさかのぼって見る渓谷美
View upstream of the inherent beauty of this gorge in the upper reaches of the Kanzaki River

滋賀県最高峰の伊吹山には、ヤマトタケル伝説が残り、白山信仰が栄えた霊峰は日本百名山の一つに数えられる
The tallest peak in Shiga Prefecture is Mt. Ibuki. It is featured in the legends of the Prince Yamato Takeru and is counted amongst Japan's Top 100 Storied Peaks because of the sanctity it commanded from ascetics.

東近江市の永源寺ダムは完成までに20年を要し、237戸が移転。その後にできたダム湖はダム湖百選に選ばれ、とりわけ紅葉の季節は素晴らしい
Eigenji Dam in Higashiomi City took 20 years to complete and forced the relocation of 237 homes. Its reservoir was later selected amongst the Top 100 Dam Reservoirs in the country and is highly reputed for the autumnal foliage.

高時川上流、長浜市余呉町菅並の集落。特別豪雪地帯に含まれている
This village is found in the upper reaches of the Takatoki River in the Suganami area of Yogocho, Nagahama City. Winters bring heavy snowfall.

　琵琶湖に流れ込む川の源は滋賀県をとりまく山々にある。水源域や流域に暮らす人々は厳しい自然と向き合いながら水の恵みに感謝し、水を大切に守り、生活に活用してきた。

The rivers flowing into Lake Biwa originate in the mountains of Shiga Prefecture. The people who live around the headwaters and in the river basin know how cruel Mother Nature can be, yet they view these water resources as blessings. Since they rely on these rivers to live, they have learned to care for them.

滋賀・びわ湖に行こう 【本書で紹介した滋賀の日本遺産】

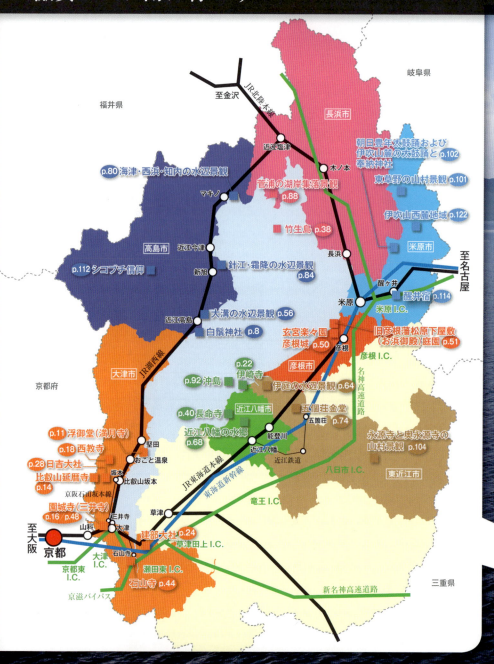

■ 公共機関で

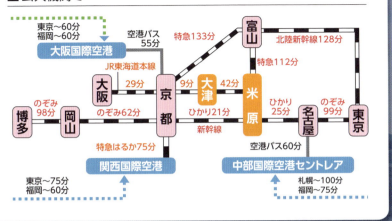

■ 車で

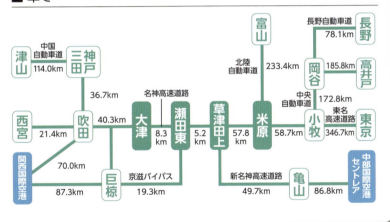

データ提供：びわこビジターズビューロー

Visit Lake Biwa, Shiga [Japan Heritages in Shiga introduced in this book]

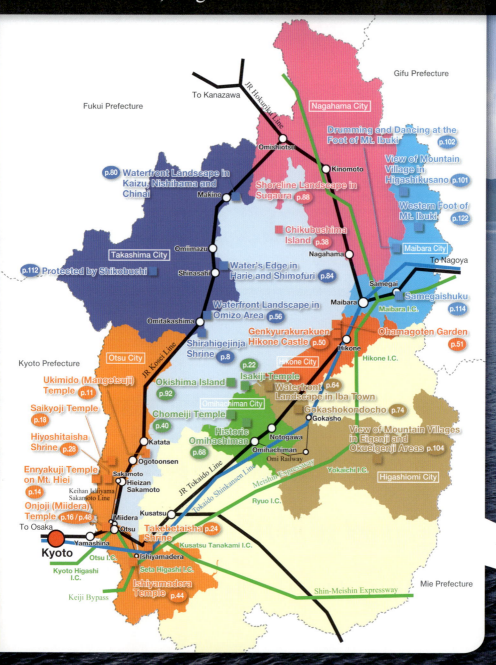

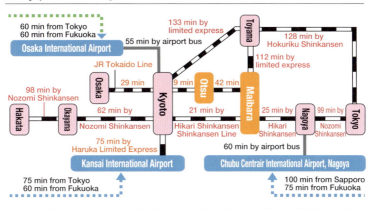

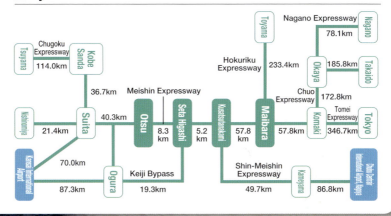

Data supplied by Biwako Visitors Bureau

Lake Biwa, Shiga
Worship and Life at Water's Edge

Copyright © Omi Culture Supporters' Club 2018
This edition published by arrangement
with Sunrise Publishing Co.,Ltd. Hikone Shiga
All right reserved.

Photographs
Tsujimura Koji

Printing
Shinano Publishing Press

近江 旅の本
滋賀・びわ湖　水辺の祈りと暮らし

2018 年 3 月 30 日　初　版　第 1 刷発行

編　集	淡海文化を育てる会
撮　影	辻村耕司
デザイン	オプティムグラフィックス
発行者	岩根順子
発行所	サンライズ出版

〒 522-0004 滋賀県彦根市鳥居本町655-1
TEL 0749-22-0627　FAX 0749-23-7720

印刷・製本　シナノパブリッシングプレス

Ⓒ Omi Culture Supporter's Club 2018　　定価はカバーに表示しております。
ISBN978-4-88325-629-7　Printed in Japan　　禁無断転載・複写